As For
ME and My
HOUSE...

A PRAYER AND DISCIPLESHIP JOURNAL

Dr. Ronnie W. Goines

Congratulations on setting your heart to COMMITTING the next 12 weeks of your life to Jesus Christ thru a discipleship/prayer journal! This is not an average daily devotional. This will require you to spend daily time with God and do some honest self-reflection. You'll also be given assignments designed to keep you rooted long after the 12 weeks have expired. Before getting started, invite a few other believers who desire to be closer with the Lord to join you. The accountability will be priceless!

The process you are about to begin is a tool that God is LITERALLY using to enhance and transform the lives of believers. While salvation grants us access to heaven upon death, discipleship grants us access to heaven while we're living. In other words, God's will is not for us to have empty, uneventful, and unauthoritative lives as we await the afterlife. But rather, we exercise Kingdom authority and relationship right now. The reality is that most Christians are not Disciples. The difference between the two will be explained at the conclusion of the following 12 weeks.

Following this brief intro you will find a commitment contract of things you commit to doing and not doing over the next 12 weeks.

12 Week Commitment

1. Believe that God will use this journal to grow you as a disciple.

2. During the entire time of this process, you must prioritize it above EVERYTHING else.

3. If you are married, inform your spouse as to what you are committing to and invite him/her to join you.

4. Abstain from drinking of any alcoholic beverages.

5. No smoking.

6. No lying. Transparency is a must.

7. No violation of any laws.

8. Abstain from sexual immorality.

9. Avoid use of profanity.

10. Set a time each day to journal.

11. Maintain status as an active member of a local church:

    - Church attendance

    - Stewardship

    - Serving in a ministry

(Note: It is strongly encouraged that you find at least one other individual to make this commitment with you.)

Date: _____ **Signature:** _____

Enjoy your journey!

WEEK 1 PRINCIPLE:

I will see life through the eyes of the person God is making me to be!

PRAYER: "Oh wise God, bless me to have spiritual 20/20 into who I am according to YOUR plan and not my past. Help me to understand how meticulously and wonderfully you've designed me to do what only I can do. Bless me so that when I look into the mirror I'm humbled and excited by who I see! Amen."

DAY 1

What would you deem to be the biggest obstacle to fulfilling this week's principle?

_____

_____

_____

_____

_____

_____

_____

_____

_____

_____

_____

_____

_____

_____

Day 2

Write a letter to God.

_____

_____

_____

_____

_____

_____

_____

_____

_____

_____

_____

_____

_____

_____

_____

_____

DAY 3

Write and Memorize Ecclesiastes 5:4-6 and explain your understanding of it.

_____

_____

_____

_____

_____

_____

_____

_____

_____

_____

_____

_____

_____

_____

_____

_____

Day 4   Date:_____

What's on your heart today?

_____

_____

_____

_____

_____

_____

_____

_____

_____

_____

_____

_____

_____

_____

_____

Day 5

Brag on yourself or share some good news!

_____

_____

_____

_____

_____

_____

_____

_____

_____

_____

_____

_____

_____

_____

_____

Day 6

Write a letter to God.

_____

_____

_____

_____

_____

_____

_____

_____

_____

_____

_____

_____

_____

_____

DAY 7   DATE:_____

Write and memorize Joshua 24:15. Share things in your past and present that
are hindrances to serving the Lord.

_____

_____

_____

_____

_____

_____

_____

_____

_____

_____

_____

_____

_____

_____

_____

_____

_____

Week 2 Principle:

I will be a thermostat, not a thermometer!

PRAYER: "Dear Lord bless me to no longer be a mere reflection of my environment/culture, but a change agent to it. You have called me to be the salt of the earth which means whatever I encounter is to be flavored to look like you! Like a master chef oh Lord, you have added me to bland and seemingly hopeless situations for Your Glory. Amen."

DAY 1   DATE:_____

What would you deem to be the biggest obstacle to fulfilling this week's principle?

_____

_____

_____

_____

_____

_____

_____

_____

_____

_____

_____

_____

_____

_____

Day 2

Write a letter to God.

_____

_____

_____

_____

_____

_____

_____

_____

_____

_____

_____

_____

_____

_____

_____

Day 3   Date:_____

Write and memorize 2 Chronicles 7:14. Explain your understanding of it.
(Note the 4 prerequisites for God to "heal the land")

_____

_____

_____

_____

_____

_____

_____

_____

_____

_____

_____

_____

_____

_____

_____

_____

DAY 4   DATE:_____

What's on your heart today?

_____

_____

_____

_____

_____

_____

_____

_____

_____

_____

_____

_____

_____

_____

_____

_____

DAY 5

Brag on yourself or share some good news!

_____

_____

_____

_____

_____

_____

_____

_____

_____

_____

_____

_____

_____

_____

_____

_____

Day 6

Write a letter to God.

_____

_____

_____

_____

_____

_____

_____

_____

_____

_____

_____

_____

_____

_____

_____

DAY 7

Write down the 4 most important people in your life and why they hold a special place in your heart.

_____

_____

_____

_____

_____

_____

_____

_____

_____

_____

_____

_____

_____

_____

_____

Week 3 Principle:

If I fail to prepare, I will be unprepared.

PRAYER: "Heavenly Father, spur me to be a better steward of my time. Make me mindful of procrastination that it not consume the time You have allotted for preparation. Give me peace when all has been done that is to be done, but don't allow me to rest when there is more that You would have me to do. Amen."

DAY 1   DATE: _____

What would you deem to be the biggest obstacle to fulfilling this week's principle?

_____

_____

_____

_____

_____

_____

_____

_____

_____

_____

_____

_____

_____

_____

_____

DAY 2

Write a letter to God.

_____

_____

_____

_____

_____

_____

_____

_____

_____

_____

_____

_____

_____

_____

DAY 3   DATE: _____

Write and memorize Matthew 6:16-18. Explain what it means to you. Do a daily 12 hour fast for the next 7 days and journal your experience.

*The Greek work for fasting "nestia" means to go without eating. Abstaining from certain activities (For example: not eating chocolate, not watching television, no internet, etc.) while are great ways to develop discipline are not the same as biblical fasting. A modified fast such as fruits and vegetables are permissible if there are health concerns to be considered.

_____

_____

_____

_____

_____

_____

_____

_____

_____

_____

_____

_____

_____

_____

Day 4

What's on your heart today?

_____

_____

_____

_____

_____

_____

_____

_____

_____

_____

_____

_____

_____

_____

DAY 5   DATE: _____

Write and memorize the Fruit of the Spirit found in Galatians 5:22-23. Which have been the hardest for you to exude and how can you be better in those areas? Remember, you have all 9 Fruit. Don't let the enemy, yourself, or your past convince you otherwise.

_____

_____

_____

_____

_____

_____

_____

_____

_____

_____

_____

_____

_____

DAY 6   DATE: _____

Write a letter to God. Be sure to write about your fasting experience so far!

_____

_____

_____

_____

_____

_____

_____

_____

_____

_____

_____

_____

_____

_____

_____

_____

DAY 7

DATE: _____

In what ways does your prayer differ from the model prayer in Matthew 6:9-13? Has fasting this week impacted your prayer life?

_____

_____

_____

_____

_____

_____

_____

_____

_____

_____

_____

_____

_____

_____

_____

_____

Week 4 Principle:

If I cannot be honest with myself I cannot be honest with God.

PRAYER: "God help me by way of the Holy Spirit that I am to be ever mindful that You know all about me and STILL love me. Make me discerning of the difference between faith and fooling myself. If the enemy has been successful in convincing me of a false reality PLEASE raise up someone that knows You and loves me enough to reveal it. Help my heart and mind be open to hear truth, even when it's uncomfortable. Amen."

DAY 1   DATE: _____

Write about a time in your life when you were not being honest with yourself
and can now see where it was hindering your walk with the Lord and others.

_____

_____

_____

_____

_____

_____

_____

_____

_____

_____

_____

_____

_____

DAY 2   DATE: _____

Write a letter to God. (If applicable, please mention how you felt on any day(s) you did not complete a full 12 hour day of fasting or not sticking with DAILY writing in your journal.)

_____

_____

_____

_____

_____

_____

_____

_____

_____

_____

_____

_____

_____

_____

_____

DAY 3   DATE: _____

Read Galatians 5:16-21. Which activity of the flesh do you struggle with and where do you think it comes from?

NOTE: The Spirit and flesh (sinful desires) are the antithesis of one another and thus are NEVER on the same side. To function "in the flesh" is literally to war against God.

_____

_____

_____

_____

_____

_____

_____

_____

_____

_____

_____

_____

DAY 4   DATE: _____

What's on your heart today?

_____

_____

_____

_____

_____

_____

_____

_____

_____

_____

_____

_____

_____

_____

_____

DAY 5

What is something that you are willing to do, or no longer do that would demonstrate your sincerity in wanting to be inside of God's will for your life?

_____

_____

_____

_____

_____

_____

_____

_____

_____

_____

_____

_____

_____

_____

_____

_____

DAY 6   DATE: _____

Share an experience you've had this week where you were not honest with
yourself, others, or God!

_____

_____

_____

_____

_____

_____

_____

_____

_____

_____

_____

_____

_____

_____

_____

Humility may be defined as strength under control. Write about a time
when you encountered an individual who defended their wrong-doing.
When did you ever do the same?

_____

_____

_____

_____

_____

_____

_____

_____

_____

_____

_____

_____

_____

Week 5 Principle:

I will sacrifice anything that prevents
me from walking with Christ!

Prayer: "Lord I realize being a discipled Christian might cost me relationships, possessions, and claims. But I count it all as rubbish that I may know you! Help me continue to valuate YOU above all else in my life that I not ever elevate gifts above the Gift Giver. Amen."

DAY 1   DATE: _____

Why might this week's principle be so hard for people to do?

_____

_____

_____

_____

_____

_____

_____

_____

_____

_____

_____

_____

_____

_____

Write a letter to God concerning what you may have the most trouble sacrificing. Include how sacrificing it would make you feel as a person, and how it
might better position you to be used by God!

_____

_____

_____

_____

_____

_____

_____

_____

_____

_____

_____

_____

_____

_____

_____

DAY 3   DATE: _____

Write and memorize John 13:34-35. Explain what makes it hard or easy for
you to express love towards others.

_____

_____

_____

_____

_____

_____

_____

_____

_____

_____

_____

_____

_____

_____

DAY 4   DATE: _____

What's on your heart today?

_____

_____

_____

_____

_____

_____

_____

_____

_____

_____

_____

_____

_____

_____

_____

_____

_____

DAY 5 　　　　　　　　　　　　　　　DATE: _____

What do you love about you, and what do others love about you? What does
God love about you?

_____

_____

_____

_____

_____

_____

_____

_____

_____

_____

_____

_____

_____

_____

DAY 6   DATE: _____

Brag on yourself or share something great going on in your life!

_____

_____

_____

_____

_____

_____

_____

_____

_____

_____

_____

_____

_____

_____

_____

_____

There are 3 voices that disciples must be able to differentiate between: their own, the devil's, and God's. How do you distinguish between them?

NOTE: Often times the voices may sound the same. Remember that the bible will disagree with the devil EVERY time, with you SOME of the time, but NEVER with God!

_____

_____

_____

_____

_____

_____

_____

_____

_____

_____

_____

_____

Week 6 Principle:

I will be there for other believers as Christ was there for me.

Prayer: "Thank you God for being the one constant in my life that has always been there for me. There were things I've told You that I wouldn't dare whisper to another. Time after time, promise after promise, mistake after mistake I've proven myself unworthy of your love; yet You keep on being way better to me than I deserve. All I can do is say THANK YOU! God give me opportunity to introduce others to this type unconditional love by loving and comforting them as you've done for me. Amen."

DAY 1   DATE: _____

What might hinder you from or spur you towards fulfilling this week's principle?

_____

_____

_____

_____

_____

_____

_____

_____

_____

_____

_____

_____

_____

_____

DAY 2   DATE: _____

Write out and memorize Galatians 6:1. Explain what it means to you.

_____

_____

_____

_____

_____

_____

_____

_____

_____

_____

_____

_____

_____

_____

_____

DAY 3   DATE: _____

Write about an instance when someone pointed out a shortcoming in your life. How did it make you feel towards that individual? Write about when you held someone accountable to either doing the right thing or to stop doing the wrong thing.

_____

_____

_____

_____

_____

_____

_____

_____

_____

_____

_____

_____

_____

_____

DAY 4   DATE: _____

What if anything are people starting to notice about you since you began this journal? How does that make you feel?

_____

_____

_____

_____

_____

_____

_____

_____

_____

_____

_____

_____

_____

_____

_____

_____

DAY 5

Write a letter to God.

_____

_____

_____

_____

_____

_____

_____

_____

_____

_____

_____

_____

_____

_____

_____

_____

_____

_____

DAY 6   DATE: _____

Devote the next 24 hours to fasting and prayer. Be sure to identify and write down key areas for prayer throughout the day. Remember prayer isn't just talking to God, but listening to Him. (Note: If you have health restrictions, please do a modified fast of fruits and vegetables only.)

_____

_____

_____

_____

_____

_____

_____

_____

_____

_____

_____

_____

_____

_____

DAY 7   DATE: _____

Write and memorize John 3:16 and Romans 10:9. Share the time you made
this confession of faith. Find an opportunity within the next 24 hours to share
this scripture with an unsaved person. (Thoroughly familiarize yourself with
Romans 10:8-17 before attempting to lead a person to Christ.)

_____

_____

_____

_____

_____

_____

_____

_____

_____

_____

_____

_____

_____

Week 7 Principle:

A bad day does not warrant a bad attitude.

Prayer: "God when things are not going according to my plan or when I'm treated unfairly, remind me that I have no right to treat others in an unloving manner. As a human I understand that every day won't be rosy, but you are worthy to be praised every day. The bottom line is that I owe You better than a bad attitude. A bad attitude can only be maintained when I'm not appreciative of all the wonderful things You've done in my life. I can't always control what type of day I'm having (or had), but I can choose to have a positive attitude with others. Whenever I'm tempted to lash out at others, PLEASE remind me of how You've never treated me in that manner. Amen."

DAY 1   DATE: _____

What are the obstacles that will hinder you from this week's principle and
how will you overcome them?

_____

_____

_____

_____

_____

_____

_____

_____

_____

_____

_____

_____

_____

_____

Day 2

Write a letter to God.

_____

_____

_____

_____

_____

_____

_____

_____

_____

_____

_____

_____

_____

_____

_____

_____

Day 3

Write out the books of the New Testament and memorize them in order.

_____

_____

_____

_____

_____

_____

_____

_____

_____

_____

_____

_____

_____

_____

_____

_____

_____

DAY 4:   DATE: _____

Write and memorize James 1:2-3, 5. What experiences come to mind?

_____

_____

_____

_____

_____

_____

_____

_____

_____

_____

_____

_____

_____

_____

_____

DAY 5   DATE: _____

Brag on yourself or share some good news!

_____

_____

_____

_____

_____

_____

_____

_____

_____

_____

_____

_____

_____

_____

_____

_____

_____

Day 6

Write a letter to God.

_____

_____

_____

_____

_____

_____

_____

_____

_____

_____

_____

_____

_____

_____

_____

DATE: _____

Write and memorize Romans 8:28. Why should this be great news for
believers?

_____

_____

_____

_____

_____

_____

_____

_____

_____

_____

_____

_____

_____

_____

_____

_____

Week 8 Principle:

Excuses are tools of incompetence that build bridges to nowhere, those who use them seldom accomplish anything.

Prayer: "Dear Lord, I celebrate the fact that through You all things are not only possible but inevitable! Forgive me for camouflaging my lack of faith in You with excuses. This week I will put into action everything I've used an excuse not to do. Though my excuses may have some merit, You tower above them. Help me in my faith to fight thru any excuse that causes me to delay or feel inept to be the person you've created me to be. Whether in education, relationships, ministry, asking for forgiveness, church attendance, stewardship, exercise, a family trip, etc., I will let no excuse deter me! Amen."

DAY 1   DATE: _____

What are the excuses you've used in the past for not doing as God would've had you do? Are you still using them?

_____

_____

_____

_____

_____

_____

_____

_____

_____

_____

_____

_____

_____

_____

_____

_____

_____

Day 2

Write a letter to God.

_____

_____

_____

_____

_____

_____

_____

_____

_____

_____

_____

_____

_____

_____

_____

Day 3   Date: _____

What are 2 things you'd love to change about yourself and why?

_____

_____

_____

_____

_____

_____

_____

_____

_____

_____

_____

_____

_____

_____

_____

_____

DAY 4   DATE: _____

Have you changed the 2 things you noted on yesterday? How did you or why
didn't you?

_____

_____

_____

_____

_____

_____

_____

_____

_____

_____

_____

_____

_____

_____

DAY 5   DATE: _____

Meditate on 2 Corinthians 12:7-10 then memorize, and journal on 2
Corinthians 12:9-10.

_____

_____

_____

_____

_____

_____

_____

_____

_____

_____

_____

_____

_____

_____

Go back and read the principle learned for Week 5. Do you have any new incite on it?

_____

_____

_____

_____

_____

_____

_____

_____

_____

_____

_____

_____

_____

_____

DATE 7   DATE: _____

Write and memorize Ephesians 3:20-21. Explain what it means to you.

_____

_____

_____

_____

_____

_____

_____

_____

_____

_____

_____

_____

_____

_____

_____

_____

Week 9 Principle:

I will preach the Gospel using words only when necessary.

Prayer: "God in a time where talk is cheap and people are looking for authenticity, show me how to live the Gospel. Through my lifestyle I pray that when others observe me they see fruit of someone who was loved, forgiven, and for whom blood was shed. Let my actions lead lost people to ask 'What must I do to be saved?' Give me the wisdom to know when it's time to bring someone to church or to be the church! I pray that when I get to heaven I'm blown away by the multitude of souls You were able to reach because I was a mime for the Gospel. Amen."

Reflect on Romans 10:9.

How might someone know that you are a Christian without you telling them? What actions may have communicated that you were not a Christian within the last 30 days?

_____

_____

_____

_____

_____

_____

_____

_____

_____

_____

_____

_____

Write a letter to God.

_____

_____

_____

_____

_____

_____

_____

_____

_____

_____

_____

_____

_____

_____

_____

_____

_____

DAY 3   DATE: _____

Write and memorize 2 Timothy 3:16-17. Do you find yourself dreading having to memorize scripture or looking forward to it? Why or why don't you feel scripture memorization is necessary?

_____

_____

_____

_____

_____

_____

_____

_____

_____

_____

_____

_____

_____

_____

_____

DAY 4   DATE: _____

Write and memorize John 1:1,14.

How does verse 14 relate to this week's principle?

_____

_____

_____

_____

_____

_____

_____

_____

_____

_____

_____

_____

_____

DAY 5

What's on your heart?

_____

_____

_____

_____

_____

_____

_____

_____

_____

_____

_____

_____

_____

_____

_____

_____

_____

DAY 6   DATE: _____

Write a letter to God.

_____

_____

_____

_____

_____

_____

_____

_____

_____

_____

_____

_____

_____

_____

_____

DAY 7   DATE: _____

Write and memorize the 10 Commandments found in Exodus 20:1-17.

_____

_____

_____

_____

_____

_____

_____

_____

_____

_____

_____

_____

_____

_____

_____

_____

_____

_____

WEEK 10 PRINCIPLE:

I will hold my brother/sister accountable even at
the risk of losing the relationship.

Prayer: "Lord most people are not comfortable with being held accountable because its often perceived as confrontation. I am called to be salt and light before a buddy. I'd much rather see a friendship end due to your truth being shared, as opposed to my silence keeping a friend and you lose a soul. Amen.""

DAY 1   DATE: _____

What persons in your life came to mind when reading this week's principle?
How might you guess they would respond to you holding them accountable?
(REMEMBER Galatians 6:1)

_____

_____

_____

_____

_____

_____

_____

_____

_____

_____

_____

_____

_____

_____

_____

_____

Day 2   Date: _____

Write a letter to God. Has is become harder or easier to write letters to God each week?

_____

_____

_____

_____

_____

_____

_____

_____

_____

_____

_____

_____

_____

_____

DAY 3   DATE: _____

Choose a person from Day 1 of this week and write a manuscript of what you'd say to them along the lines of holding them accountable. (Use Galatians 6:1 as a point of reference)

_____

_____

_____

_____

_____

_____

_____

_____

_____

_____

_____

_____

_____

_____

_____

_____

DAY 4   DATE: _____

Write and memorize Proverb 15:1 and Psalm 133:1.

_____

_____

_____

_____

_____

_____

_____

_____

_____

_____

_____

_____

_____

_____

_____

DAY 5

What's on your heart?

_____

_____

_____

_____

_____

_____

_____

_____

_____

_____

_____

_____

_____

_____

_____

_____

_____

Day 6

Write a letter to God.

_____

_____

_____

_____

_____

_____

_____

_____

_____

_____

_____

_____

_____

_____

_____

_____

DAY 7   DATE: _____

Read Proverbs 7 in its entirety. Is there or has there ever been a person in your
life that fits this description? Have you ever fit this description?

_____

_____

_____

_____

_____

_____

_____

_____

_____

_____

_____

_____

_____

_____

_____

_____

_____

_____

Week 11 Principle:

Resentment towards my brother/sister in Christ is spiritual suicide.

Prayer: "Lord it's hard to not hold grudges and be resentful at times when I've really been treated unfairly. Help me to forgive others how You constantly forgive me. Don't let me become comfortable with the resentment I may be harboring in my heart, even if I'm able to justify it. Rather than patience to 'put up' with those I don't care for, give me the compassion to serve them. Amen".

Write about a present or past situation in your life where you know this principle to be true.

_____

_____

_____

_____

_____

_____

_____

_____

_____

_____

_____

_____

_____

_____

_____

_____

DAY 2   DATE: _____

Write a letter to God.

_____

_____

_____

_____

_____

_____

_____

_____

_____

_____

_____

_____

_____

_____

_____

_____

DAY 3

What does 1 Corinthians 3:16 mean to you? How might proper exercise and diet correlate to this scripture?

_____

_____

_____

_____

_____

_____

_____

_____

_____

_____

_____

_____

_____

_____

_____

Have you sought out the person you noted from last week's Day 3 to fulfill the principle from that week? If so, what happened?

_____

_____

_____

_____

_____

_____

_____

_____

_____

_____

_____

_____

_____

_____

Day 5

What's on your heart?

_____

_____

_____

_____

_____

_____

_____

_____

_____

_____

_____

_____

_____

_____

_____

_____

_____

Day 6

Write God a letter.

_____

_____

_____

_____

_____

_____

_____

_____

_____

_____

_____

_____

_____

_____

_____

_____

DAY 7   DATE: _____

Share how challenging and rewarding journaling over the last 11 weeks has been for you.

_____

_____

_____

_____

_____

_____

_____

_____

_____

_____

_____

_____

_____

_____

_____

_____

Week 12 Principle:

I will be Spiritually motivated not emotionally attached!

Prayer: "Lord the only way I can keep from being tossed to and fro is to not be led by my emotions. I only want the job, relationship and situation that You desire for my life. Remind me that my emotions are not always loyal to the plan You have for my life. I declare You to be my God, not my emotions or thoughts! I realize that an emotionally led life is one of constant volatility. Amen".

DAY 1   DATE: _____

Give your interpretation and personal experience concerning this week's principle.

_____

_____

_____

_____

_____

_____

_____

_____

_____

_____

_____

_____

_____

DAY 2

Write a letter to God.

_____

_____

_____

_____

_____

_____

_____

_____

_____

_____

_____

_____

_____

_____

_____

_____

Day 3

Write yourself an encouraging letter for the times in the future when you may consider giving up on something that God has called you to.

_____

_____

_____

_____

_____

_____

_____

_____

_____

_____

_____

_____

_____

_____

DAY 4   DATE: _____

Write and memorize John 3:16-18. Why are verses 17 & 18 just as important
as verse 16.

_____

_____

_____

_____

_____

_____

_____

_____

_____

_____

_____

_____

_____

_____

_____

_____

Write a manuscript of what you'd want read at your funeral. LITERALLY!
Be specific.

_____

_____

_____

_____

_____

_____

_____

_____

_____

_____

_____

_____

_____

_____

_____

_____

_____

DATE: _____

What are you Spiritually resolved to always do or never do, that supersedes your emotions? (The thing you are committed to despite how you feel.)

_____

_____

_____

_____

_____

_____

_____

_____

_____

_____

_____

_____

_____

_____

_____

Day 7

Read through your journal from Day 1 and make your final entry.

_____

_____

_____

_____

_____

_____

_____

_____

_____

_____

_____

_____

_____

_____

_____

_____

_____

Congratulations, on dedicating the last 12 weeks of your life to praying, self reflection and learning scriptures. You have initiated a process that goes far beyond just being a Christian. Jesus's instructions in the Great Commission wasn't that we go make Christians, but that we go make disciples. Salvation is free, but discipleship costs. The lack of discipleship opportunities has resulted in millions of believers living in hell on their way to heaven.

Most of those who complete this journal has done so alongside others within a group setting that honed in on fellowship, transparency, service, and accountability! That curriculum is included in the book entitled "As For Me & My House...A Discipleship Curriculum For Men". While the book addresses issues directly associated with Christian men becoming disciples, the process is applicable to women as well.

To stay sharp, this 12 week process should become an annual journey that you embark upon each year with the Lord! Keep a file for your journals through out the years, so you can look and track your growth as a disciple.

LAST ASSIGNMENT: Read John 13:1-17 then pray for the Holy Spirit to lead you to a person(s) to do what Jesus did in that text!

CPSIA information can be obtained
at www.ICGtesting.com
Printed in the USA
FSOW03n1207191115
13588FS